Hugh Flattery

The Pope and the new Crusade

Hugh Flattery

The Pope and the new Crusade

ISBN/EAN: 9783743344884

Manufactured in Europe, USA, Canada, Australia, Japa

Cover: Foto ©ninafisch / pixelio.de

Manufactured and distributed by brebook publishing software
(www.brebook.com)

Hugh Flattery

The Pope and the new Crusade

The Pope
and the
New Crusade

BY

POLYBIUS

The Pope

and

The New Crusade

BY

POLYBIUS

Os Leonis Os Petri

"ΕΙΣ ΚΟΙΡΑΝΟΣ ΕΣΤΩ."
—*Iliad, ii.*, 204.

NEW YORK

THOMAS R. KNOX & CO.

SUCCESSORS TO JAMES MILLER

817 BROADWAY

TROW'S
PRINTING AND BOOKBINDING COMPANY,
NEW YORK.

I.

THE POPE AND THE NEW CRUSADE.

I.

Philanthropic feats benign
We relate, oh! Tuneful Nine,
To galvanize this sick, lethargic land and
age!
Scatter opulence broadcast—
Hoodlums, cobblers at the last—
Come, toiling crowds, participate our mission
sage!

II.

Hidden truths shall we reveal,
Mystic laws boldly unseal,
Erstwhile clos'd to all misgovern'd sons of
Eve!
Nature's bounties spread apace—
Cataractic floods of grace
Perennial flow on who our craze sublime be-
lieve!

III.

Theories sophistical,
Mephistophelistical—
Far from pre-Adamic nations fresh imported,
The primordial chaos
(At the millionnaire's sole loss)
To the poor man's balance-sheet straightway
transported !

IV.

By our potent magic wand
We'll so reinvest the land
Sobs and groans, like Egypt's plagues, 'll flee
before us !
Then, in patriarchal ways,
Happy lisp life's laughing lays,
Enchanted nature disenthrall'd, resume the
chorus !

V.

Jovian paternity !
Georgian fraternity !
Ho ! clear the way for " The Cross of the New
    Crusade !"
  " No Pov'rty Society"
  (Grab unto satiety)—
Zounds ! nor land, nor light, nor—moonshine,
    by man was made !

VI.

Our saving Cross—an axe,
Our supreme law—no tax,
Go blissful bask in sunlit bowers all life long !
  " The sanctity of labor "
  (The fair Eve's apple savor,)
It ringeth blithely as king rooster's matin
    song !

VII.

Bucolic creed Dianian,
Herbaceous—all Arcadian—
Knight-toilers Æolian evangel reverent!
    Oh ! tender tulip teacher,
    Oh ! pretty pansy preacher,
Archimandrite of the " unearned increment !"

VIII.

In the sweat upon thy brow
(Spake the One Eternal Now)
Curst ! shalt thou eat the bread of life till life's
        a blank ?
    Pshaw ! superstitious trader
    (Glosseth our arch crusader—
Awry bear of Pennsylvania's mountebank !)

IX.

Ah! grim, hybrid alliance—
Mongrel twin-apes of science
List! they've seized the tail of the scientific eel!
Ay! dupe brainless multitudes—
Cads, cranks, callous spinsters, dudes!
Ye doom'd denizens of stern Uncle Sam's bas-
tile!

X.

Ills of Capital ye fight
(Only $75.00 per night!)
Rome's Capitol was sav'd by half seventy
geese!
To bamboozle the masses
Go in to scalp the classes—
Alack! rich, poor, high, low, amuck go on to
fleece!

XI.

Swift swells big golden " divvy,"
Now sport the gay "Tantivy "
Tally-ho ! thro' hill and dell, heigh ! Faugha-
    balaugh !
Sancho Panza George for "whip,"
Ev'ry mile the cheering "nip,"
Homing, wreathe the foaming bowl—in Pov'rty
    Hollow !

XII.

Peter's piscatorial hook,
Temper'd fine in Kedron's brook,
Greek George nerv'd of old to bag the slimy
    Dragon ;
Ha ! th' anglers of our Zion
Fish wide of Tiber's Lion,
Ho ! dragoon'd they drive Old Harry's mar-
    ket wagon !

XIII.

Behold the New Creation!
Fat, frothy declamation,
Neoplastic, black, de-Christianiz'd Labarum!
Of belov'd " disciple " blest
(Oh ! ye gods, give us a rest !)
Ghastly shade of ghostly "Judices Cau-
sarum ! "

●

II.

THE CRUSADER TO THE POPE.

I.

Hail, High Pontiff! from afar
Come I, not to carry war
'Gainst the rock that pulverizeth kings and
  sages,
But to fix the Pope's own eyes
On th' abysmal truth that lies
In great Henry George's rich-embroider'd
  pages!

II.

In fact, Most Holy Father,
You need advice the rather—
That mere garbl'd information prepossesses ;
Even lofty minds like yours,
Nay, at times mayhap obscures—
The which your countless loving sons sore
  distresses.

III.

In American affairs
There's a set of millionnaires—
Gosh! they want to ride it rough-shod o'er
    the masses!
So myself and Henry George
Weapons engineer'd to forge
Once for all to "put a head" upon the classes!

.

IV.

What with gross fatuity,
Wanton ambiguity,
Weeping millions of the people outcasts
    hurl'd!
Laws in fallacies founded,
By judges base expounded,
The whole fabric of society's imperill'd!

V.

Customs, usages clean wrong,
Government itself a song,
Oh ! bless this " New Crusade "—all sorrow's
   panacea !
Give knaves, rogues, intrig'ing swarms,
   "Their belly full of reforms ; "
No fabl'd sucklings we of lupine priestess
   Rhea.

VI.

Fancy not we're quite so green
As to worship "the machine "
Of your singularly " mixed " administration ;
   Nor diplomatic fakirs,
   Nor toged mischief-makers,
Can our end achieve—mankind's emancipa-
   tion !

VII.

Far more papal than the Pope,
We'll not give the rich free rope—
Our wage-winning hosts t' enslave on bread
          and water;
Rather win unique renown,
Samsonize New York's old town,
Hail! Neroic, Roman holiday of slaughter!

VIII.

Just to our plans pray " tumble,"
Nor be cajol'd to stumble.
Lo! we'll revive the halcyon days of Mother
          Church !
But by Matthew, Mark, Luke, John,
If our cause you frown upon,
We'll leave Pope, Vatican, Prop'ganda in the
          lurch !

IX.

Let Rome's Pontiff understand
Mighty Heaven made the land
For all Noah's sons' delight and common
   glory !
  Lest some " club " from West'rn
   shores
  Wi' rough, rugged, roofless pores—
Tom'hawk "th' old gentleman's stove-pip'd
   upper story ! "

X.

  Put an apostolic ban !
  On the liberties of man !
In Manhattan's sea-girt citadel of freedom !
  Harp in harmonious staves,
  With tough Tammany's brusque braves !
Bones of Franklin ! this is resurrecting
   Tweedom !

XI.

"Compensation !—not a penny ! "
(What ! tak'st me for a Jenny ?)
Unto the heartless, "miscall'd owners of the
soil ! "
Let the rich wax richer still ?
Let the poor man tread the mill ?
Great Scott ! it makes my blood like 'Frisco's
geysers boil !

XII.

Strong behind us are the "Knights"
(Ahem! O'Brien's "black-eye" frights—)
You bet they capture, sure, next Presidential
vote ;
Mark ! I've given you the hint,
In this matter there's a mint,
Your man to Washington our "wave" 'll sure-
ly float.

XIII.

With this choice evangel true,
We bid Your Holiness—adieu !
Remember, prithee ! we are nearing fast the
　　" Fall."
Whosoever trusts in me,
Says good-by to poverty—
Well ! see you later on *the* question—
　　"AFTER ALL."

III.

THE POPE TO THE CRU-SADER.

I.

Now, good Doctor, quoth the Pope,
We can give thee no soft soap
(As to far-famed Blarney Castle—We ne'er
    saw it ;)
Unto us it clear appears,
Thou art boxing thine own ears,
While thy headless doct'ral cap—shame ! why
    so paw it ?

II.

Thy stale sophisms We've conn'd
    well,
Calm, unsway'd by warping spell—
In the empyrean vision of CHIEF PASTOR ;
And we notify thee, hark !
To collide with Peter's bark
Means, on this and yonder shore, supreme
    disaster.

III.

In Our peerless Urban school,
Learned'st not how to keep cool ?
Alas ! full quick wayward urchins dodge their
lessons !
Head and heart alike soon turn,
Into scorpions that burn—
Such reckless priests curses spread instead of
" blessin's."

IV.

" Emancipate all labor ! "
False, fribble, sly palaver—
Crude, rancid cantWe loathe as simply bestial :
On thy soul a golden brand,
Hold ! bespatterest with sand !
Priests should soar to higher regions all celes-
tial !

V.

Why not embark in letters ?
Break culture's iron fetters ?
Go to sea ? or shoulder arms ? or something
    bigger ?
Or exploit some winsome part
In the fairy realms of Art ?
Why descend so low to play coarse cellar-
    digger ?

VI.

Give up mock Theology,
Take up Ichthyology,
In due course, we ween, they'll acclaim thee
    Doctor Fish !
But within the Master's House,
List ! no tricky, vicious chouse
May chaos breed. Beware ! only themselves
    such dish.

VII.

Thy extremely shallow pate
Would depict all real estate
As a cancer in the bowels of creation—
Would enthrone State despotism
Above rank absolutism
By a weird, barbaric scheme of confiscation.

VIII.

Would'st depose the gang in power,
Far viler elves t' embower,
'Mid luscious plums of fragrant pelf and
plunder ;
In spurious indignation,
Cast dust all o'er the nation,
Ha   entomb a Continent in blood and thun-
der.

IX.

Pray, is government a myth ?
Rather, is it not the pith
Of wickedness in demented men t' ambition,
    Under pretence of "reform,"
    T' arouse a ruinous storm,
Then pluck th' "unearned increment" of po-
    sition ?

X.

God rained down upon the land,
The sweat of thy father's hand ;
Wretch ! when face down'r'd, cross his knees
    he spank'd thee well,
    All too soon th' old man let up—
    Christians sip the wormwood cup.
Arise, avenger ! worm remorse ! ope gaping
    Hell !

XI.

Blaze th' incendiary's fuse !
What have murd'rous cranks to lose ?
Without honor, credit, fortune, reputation !
Homes of happiness ignite ?
Plenty, peace, and progress blight ?
Crushing myriad guileless hearts in desola-
tion !

XII.

What ! thinkest, in sooth, to sham
That grave Mentor—Uncle Sam ?
In loyal son, ah me ! parricidal raking !
But We'll show, before We've done,
Thy mental web's too thin spun—
Thieves oft twist their own death-couch in
halter-making.

XIII.

Our late predecessor's feet,
With unbounded love to greet,
Came pilgrims from all States of great Colum-
  bia—
To revere this See of Sees,
They defied proud Neptune's sneeze
(We were then a plain Archbishop down in
  Umbria.)

XIV.

Nay, long centuries before,
Tell historians galore
(Unto no nation Primal Chair deigns to pan-
  der,)
When the jealous Portuguese,
Fain 'd thwart *the* Genoese,
Say, Doctor mine ! who drew the line ? Pope
  Alexander !

XV.

Nor floats abroad, unfurl'd,
In this vast, majestic world
(Our own undimm'd Tiara greets her lustrous
        Stars !)
One flag in whose ample fold
Pontiff, prelates, people hold—
Such Stripes to lash the frenzied votaries of
        Mars !

XVI.

Touching Mr. Buncombe George
(Chatter-boxes must disgorge)
'Tis writ—How keep his fingers clean that
        toucheth pitch ?
Even school-boys understand,
As 'twixt law and lifeless land,
" Can the blind lead the blind "—save into the
        ditch ?

XVII.

What alliance with the spade,
Hath the ministerial blade
Of Christ's generals high empow'r'd to lead
    the fold?
Trail the altar in the dust?
Burn incense to the lust?
Of monstrous firebrands whose sole god is
    filthy gold?

XVIII.

Then beloved, erring child
(We would breathe but accents mild,)
Ponder deep that thrice-blest day of Ordina-
    tion!
When the Pentecostal Dove
'Spous'd thy soul in hallow'd love—
Mystic Lamb t' immolate in clean oblation.

XIX.

From a Pontiff's heart immense,
T'ward all weaklings void of sense,
To Him who purg'd of old Isaiah's lips with
fire,
Our best orisons ascend
Thy odd, hircic ways to mend,
Magdalene's tears and stout resolve thy breast
inspire.

XX.

Avaunt ! Plutonic nitre !
Revere thy Bishop's mitre,
See the lowly, gentle, graceful, drooping
osier !
Humbly bow thy stubborn neck,
Scandal's turbid torrent check,
Else depart ! with deathless smart of
PETER'S CROZIER !!!

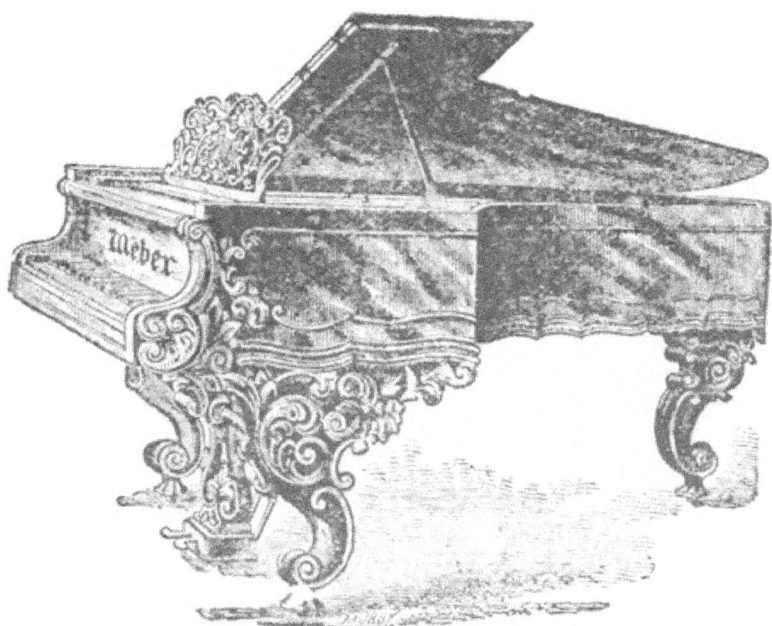

STYLE 1.—7¼ OCTAVES.

Rosewood Upright or Boudoir Piano.

Overstrung Scale, Three Strings, Patent Action, $650.

Height, 4 feet 1¼ inches; width, 4 feet 9 inches; depth, 2 feet 2 inches

To the Public:

To enable parties who are desirous of purchasing a really *first-class* instrument, but are unable to pay cash in full for same, we will, during the *next three months*, sell the above instrument for $425, delivered free of charge within twenty-five miles of our warehouse, on the following terms: $100 cash, balance in monthly installments of $25. We should be pleased to have you make us a call.

WAREROOMS: Fifth Avenue, corner West 16th Street,

NEW YORK CITY.

•

www.ingramcontent.com/pod-product-compliance
Lightning Source LLC
Chambersburg PA
CBHW021445090426
42739CB00009B/1644